Gymnastics

Have you watched gymnasts flying
through the air like birds from high
apparatus? What must it feel like and
how can you be trained to do
gymnastics? Many young people who
are already good at this sport will enjoy
this book, and others may want to
begin.

InterSport

Gymnastics

David Hunn

**Colour photographs by
Tony Duffy
All-Sport Limited**

Wayland/Silver Burdett

InterSport

The world of international sport seen through
the cameras of some of the world's greatest
sports photographers, showing in action both
children and the stars they admire.

Motocycling
Soccer
Tennis
Track and Field

Cycling
Golf
Gymnastics
Ice Sports

Frontispiece **Who to Watch?** – Unlike most sports,
gymnastics championships often have many different
events happening at the same time. It is sometimes a
difficult choice for the spectators to decide who to watch!

First published in 1980 by Wayland Publishers Limited
49 Lansdowne Place, Hove, East Sussex BN3 1HF, England
© Copyright Wayland Publishers Limited
ISBN 0 85340 771 1

Published in the United States by Silver Burdett Company, Morristown, New Jersey
1980 Printing
ISBN 0382 06424–0

Phototypeset by Trident Graphics Limited, Reigate, Surrey
Printed in Italy by G. Canale & C.S.p.A., Turin

Contents

Beginnings

For many millions of television viewers across the world, gymnastics began with Olga Korbut, the little Russian girl who captured the hearts of those who saw her perform at Munich in the 1972 Olympic Games. It was Korbut who caused the queues to form at gymnastics clubs all over Britain and America. Four years later, people were spellbound by Nadia Comaneci, Olympic champion at only 14. Gymnastics became popular in the 1970s, although it has been practised for many years, particularly in the eastern countries of the world.

We can't all be Olga Korbuts or Nadia Comanecis, but you don't have to be perfect to enjoy gymnastics. At first, you need to be bold and agile. Then, with practice, the boys become stronger and the girls become more graceful. Nothing is more important than that you really enjoy what you are doing and try your hardest to do it well.

Beam Splits — Tiny, cheeky Maria Filatova of the USSR, who won the 1977 World Cup, shows all the balance, concentration and extraordinary flexibility of a top-rate gymnast.

Vaulting

You wouldn't be reading this book if you did not think that gymnastics is fun. That does not mean you don't have to concentrate to do it well. You do – all the time and very hard, shutting out of your mind everything except the exercise you are working on.

It is not too difficult to keep up concentration because the vault is over so quickly. You have to pack all your energy and concentration into a tight bundle as you stand at the end of the run and then let it escape as you run up to the springboard – not in an explosion, but in a smooth roar like a train rushing through a short tunnel.

Your run up to the springboard is very important as you cannot vault well unless you can run fast. Watch the marvellous Soviet girls sprinting to the vaulting horse and you see the energy and determination bursting out of them with every step – they look as if they could run through the horse and the wall beyond it! Actually every step is carefully measured out so that they should land exactly where they want to on the springboard.

Power and Precision — The approach and vault on to the 'long horse' (used by male gymnasts) has to be perfectly measured as the gymnast is travelling at full speed. Here the outstanding American Kurt Thomas is fully extended to reach the 'neck' of the horse.

In the simple straddle and squat vaults with which gymnastics begins, the hands and arms do not have much work to do. In competitions, women and girls always vault over the broad horse – that is, the length of the horse is facing them. Men and older boys have to use the long horse; the horse is turned the other way round so that the tail end, or croup, is facing them and they have much further to travel in their flight to clear the horse. To plan getting over, they divide it up in their minds into three sections – the croup, the saddle and the neck. The hands must land on the right part of the horse.

But the vault is not over once you have sprung above the horse. The more advanced vaults begin to get exciting at this moment. All the power built up in the run and take-off is directed by the muscles of the arms and shoulders to send the body into spectacular twists, turns and somersaults in the air.

Dizzy Heights — It's hard to believe that Elizo Kenmotsu of Japan achieved this height by a somersault from a horse!

What Next? — The audience holds its breath in anticipation as Gitta Escher *(left)* of East Germany sails through the air towards the 'broad horse' used by female gymnasts. The most exciting and spectacular twists, turns and somersaults are to be seen once the gymnast has touched the horse.

Floor exercises

You are all alone in the floor exercises – just you and a 12 metre (40 ft) square mat. There is no apparatus to help or hinder you, and both boys and girls have the chance to display individual style and ability with greater freedom than in any other event. The girls' exercises are the most popular part of any gymnastics programme.

The girls are lucky because they do their routine to music. Most of them love being able to dance to a favourite piece, carefully chosen to suit their personality and show their ability to the best advantage. The rules no longer insist on one instrument only, and performers are now allowed to use orchestrated music.

Mental control is as important as physical training. The competitor must concentrate all the time and be able to think herself carefully through each stage or step. So if the floor exercises look simple when performed by the great gymnasts, it has only come through hard work. Though it looks so free you cannot just do what you like on the floor. For the women's compulsory exercises at the

She Who Won the Hearts of Millions — Olga Korbut of the USSR inspired gymnasts throughout the world by her performances during the 1972 Munich Olympics. Her extraordinary skill and enchanting personality turned gymnastics into one of the most popular spectator sports.

12

Montreal Olympics in 1976 there were eighty detailed instructions to be memorized.

Boys' exercises tend to be less beautiful than those of the girls, but they are perhaps more exciting. As well as showing how athletic and agile they can be, boys particularly demonstrate strength and balance.

A show of strength is discouraged in the girls' event. Their performance must contain aspects of basic dancing (most female gymnasts have ballet lessons) and the judges award points for a blend of graceful body movement, personality and gymnastic skill.

Personality has become very important. When Ludmilla Tourischeva won her Olympic, World and European titles, she scored points for the exquisite beauty of her movements and her superb gymnastic artistry. But it was the elfin Olga Korbut who won the public's heart with the force of her dazzling and cheeky personality, shown at its best in her movements on the floor.

Strength and Balance — Male gymnasts are given the opportunity to display their athleticism during the floor exercises. Their programme, although less artistic than those performed by the girls, is full of exciting somersaults which demonstrate their agility. Here Alexander Detiatin *(left)* of the USSR shows both perfect balance and an awareness of the size of the 12 metre (40 ft) square mat on which the exercises are performed.

Grace and Beauty — Elena Moukhina *(right)* shows the beauty of the women's floor exercises. Most girl gymnasts have ballet lessons which help them express their skill and personality with the utmost grace.

The beam

This exercise is for girls. What can you do on the balance beam? The answer is, nearly everything that you have learned on the floor. Except, of course, you must remember that the beam is only 10.16 cm (4 in) wide, so you need plenty of nerve and courage as well as complete control of balance.

Troubles can start right at the beginning. Each routine begins with the competitor having to get on to the bar, which is 1.2 m (3 ft 11 in) off the ground. If she mounts badly, it can affect the rest of her performance.

Once she is safely on the beam, she keeps control of her balance by holding her body tight. Have you ever noticed gymnasts doing this? Learning to balance can be rewarding as well as being fun. It gives a person grace, poise and confidence.

All gymnasts have a few falls. They practise new routines on a line painted on the floor which is the same width as the beam, and they learn tumbling movements on a low bench with plenty of mats round it.

As they gain confidence, they move on to the regular beam and at first learn to walk

Faith and Courage — Ute Maiwald of West Germany displays perfect faith in her own ability as she performs a somersault on the narrow beam.

First Steps — The club coach lends a hand to balance a beginner on the beam. *(right)*.

16

on it until they can walk as naturally on the beam as they do on the ground. Once the gymnast is confident, she can go through routines on the bar, which must include graceful dance steps and tumbling movements which look very difficult to accomplish. A 'spotter' stands near the apparatus to catch anyone who falls – even the famous gymnasts have a spotter close by when they practise.

Grace and rhythm are important, but marks are awarded for 'elements of difficulty' and the way in which they are performed. The exercise must last between 75 and 95 seconds, and if the competitor falls she must remount within 10 seconds. The jump-off is just as important as the mount.

Nadia Comaneci is at her best on the beam and she scored three 'perfect' marks for this event in the 1976 Olympics.

Gaining Confidence — Balancing seems a lot easier when the beam is close to the ground! Only when these youngsters can walk as naturally on the bench as they do on solid ground will they progress to the high beam which is 1.2 m (3 ft 11 in) off the ground.

18

Asymmetric bars

It is hard to think of anything more thrilling to watch than the world-famous female gymnasts working their routines on the asymmetric bars (sometimes called the uneven bars). They swing, turn and catch like monkeys at the zoo and when they dismount, they seem to fly like birds. It takes a lot of courage.

It is perhaps the hardest of all the exercises. All the body strength is put to work and the long hours of practice strengthening the back, shoulders and arms pay off.

There was a time when girls used the same parallel bars as the men. Then someone had the bright idea of using the bars at different heights. Now the higher bar is 2.3 m (7 ft 6 in) off the ground and the lower bar is 1.5 m (4 ft 11 in) high. The gap between them can be altered to suit the gymnast.

The exercise includes swinging and circling, flight from one bar to the other, twisting, turning and springing. The gymnast must not pause and 'pose' on the bars. Flowing movement is important, but an unnecessary swing of the legs can lose

What Does It Feel Like? — Newcomers to the gym club 'get the feel' of the high and low bars. A beginner will normally learn the swinging movements — which are so essential to the assymetric bars — on a single bar at first.

marks. For a good performance, the gymnast will need the grace and agility she displayed on the floor; the speed she put into her vault; and the balance she learned for the beam.

A beginner will learn the swinging movements on a single bar at first. There will be plenty of thick mats on the floor and a spotter close by to catch her if she falls. She may have trouble with her hands until she has learned when to grip tight and when to release. The movement of the palms on the bars causes blisters and makes them sore at first. There are special hand straps to help prevent this. It is important to start wearing straps at the beginning and most famous gymnasts wear them all the time. Gymnasts chalk absorbs perspiration so that the hands will not slip.

In Flight — Time is frozen by the camera as Gitta Escher of East Germany changes her bar grip in mid-air.

Almost Beyond Belief! —Nadia Comeneci of Romania performs one of her unique straddle somersaults over the top bar. The asymmetric bars are perhaps the hardest of all the exercises performed by the female gymnast as they require all the grace and agility of the floor exercises, the speed and fluent power of the vault, and the balance of the beam.

High bar

Many people think that the high bar is the showpiece of gymnastics. The exercise is performed on a steel horizontal bar which can be as high as 2.55 m (8 ft 5 in) – higher than any other bars used in gymnastics. On this piece of equipment, male gymnasts have the chance to put on a brief but spectacular display of swinging, circling and twisting. It ends in a dismount that is often the most exciting moment of the whole gymnastics competition.

The high bar was invented by the German gymnast, Kurt Jahn, more than one hundred years ago. Like much of the equipment he introduced into gymnastics, the bar was first used to demonstrate strength as well as the swing. Today it is used only for swinging movements and a competitor is not allowed to include any move that can be accomplished by strength alone.

But what fantastic swings they are! The routine is always vigorous with a ceaseless

In the Swing — A Canadian competitor *(left)* in the World Championships shows a perfect leg posture during his high bar exercise.

flow of movement. It includes full circle swings (arms at full stretch, sometimes called giant wheels), circles in support positions (with the bar at the hips), as well as hangs and twists. Hand grips are particularly important. The success of each circle and twist depends on the hands being in the right position. The beginner has to master this skill early in his training, so that he can change quickly and with ease from a regular grip (or overgrip, with palms facing forward on to the bar) to a reverse grip (or undergrip, in which the palms face the gymnast).

The dismount is the climax of the show. Great gymnasts often leave the bar travelling up and away at high speed. This gives them the height they need to perform double and triple somersaults before they touch the floor, hopefully standing on both feet. This flight can be extremely dangerous unless the gymnast has perfect control over the timing of his departure from the bar, and the force of his landing on the floor.

Defying Gravity — Former World Champion Shigeru Kasamatsu of Japan shows perfect control during his dismount from the high bar. It's hard to believe that he is flying through the air at incredible speed!

The rings

There is something about the rings that makes them unusually difficult pieces of apparatus for the gymnast. Touch them and they move. They hang 2.5 m (8 ft 2 in) off the ground from a frame 5.5 m (17 ft 11 in) high. The gymnast's main problem is to develop the exceptional shoulder strength needed to hold them firm. It is not surprising that this is a male event only.

Although the origin of the gymnastic rings was the circus trapeze bar, on which loops and twists were performed, the rings were first used to show strength rather than swinging ability. Then, in the 1952 Olympics, gymnasts from the USSR performed 'the wheel' for the first time, swinging the body round and round between the rings. Today the event still gives the gymnast an opportunity to exercise his strength, but he cannot become a top-class competitor unless he can swing fluently and be very flexible in his muscles.

A Question of Strength —Haroji Kajiyama of Japan shows how to 'hold the crucifix', one of the most physically demanding positions in all gymnastics.

There are two movements of pure strength that are practised on the rings. One is the handstand, and the other – if the gymnast can manage it – is 'the crucifix'. The crucifix is an almost unbelievable position in which the gymnast hangs with his arms horizontally to each side and with the rings at shoulder level. Some gymnasts, even very good ones, never master this position.

The general aim in each routine is to present a succession of positions showing flexibility as well as strength, with each movement flowing in to the next one rather than jerking in to it. The 'links' between movements need to be practised as much as the movements themselves.

The gymnast's body is said to be either in 'hang' or in 'support', whether it is swinging or demonstrating strength. Hang is when the body is mostly below the vital bit of equipment; support is when the body is mostly above it, when the performer has pulled himself up between the rings and is holding himself there by the strength of his upper arms and shoulders. You only have to look at the degree of effort on the face of a gymnast to decide whether you are watching a great one or just a good one.

No Sign Of Strain — The great gymnasts perform even the most impressive manoeuvres with apparent ease. Here World Cup Bronze medallist Stoyan Deltchev of Bulgaria holds an inventive and demanding 'support' position.

The pommel horse

Two thousand years ago, Roman soldiers used a wooden horse to practise mounting and dismounting. Medieval knights used it in just the same way. Today it is used in gymnastics for exercises on the vaulting horse and the pommel horse. We have already seen how the vaulting horse is used in the second chapter.

The pommel horse is the same length as the vaulting horse, but it has a pair of handles fixed across it which the gymnast uses to support his weight. He is not allowed to touch any part of the horse except with his hands. Like the vaulting horse, the pommel horse is divided up into three parts – the croup, the saddle and the neck – which must all be used in the exercise.

The exercise must be constant movement with no pauses – no hold should last more than two seconds. It has to be performed at the same speed throughout and if the speed becomes uneven, marks will be lost. This demands a great deal of strength in the gymnast's shoulders and arms. The weight is

Only Hands! — One of the world's greatest experts on the pommel horse, Detiatin of the USSR, shows perfect control. A gymnast is not allowed to touch any part of the horse except with his hands.

supported on one or the other of the handles, while the legs and hips are swinging alongside and over the horse. Sometimes even great experts like Andrianov and Detiatin of the USSR slow down and brush the side of the horse with their legs.

If you watch one of the great gymnasts on the pommel horse – you will see how he tries to swing his whole body without ever losing his balance. It takes a lot of practice to be perfect at this exercise. Watch him circling, 'travelling' and turning his body over the horse. The Japanese, who are probably the best in the world on the pommel horse, believe it takes years to develop this skill fully. So don't be put off if you fail at first.

Travelling Light — The style and grace of 'travelling' as displayed by Bart Conner of America!

The parallel bars

More than a century ago, Kurt Jahn – the 'father' of Olympic gymnastics – invented the parallel bars, mainly to strengthen the shoulder muscles. There was strong opposition to the bars from people who believed they could deform the body. Now most people agree that there is no better place for a boy to begin serious work.

In competition, the bars are 1.75 m (5 ft 8½ in) high, but for practising they can be lowered to suit the young gymnast, so you do not have to worry too much about falling off them. Since they were invented, they have become thinner and more flexible.

Officially only one move of strength should be shown and competitors are careful to plan a routine that moves freely and smoothly above and below the bar. The performer often swings up in to handstands and even somersaults from one handstand to another.

It takes a little of everything to perform well on the parallel bars. The gymnast needs balance from practising on the pommel horse, strength from exercising with the rings, the nerve has gained on the high bar

Fingertip Control — Vladimir Markelov (USSR) looks almost weightless as he changes position above the parallel bars.

Muscle Power —A half-lever on the parallel bars brings out the best in another magnificent Soviet athlete, Alexander Tkachev.

and the explosive action he used to vault. The good all-round gymnast is definitely a favourite on this piece of apparatus. In four out of six Olympic Games up to 1976, the overall champion in gymnastics has been the man who won the parallel bars.

Making a Start — Only two out of ten for style, but these East German boys are discovering the delights of the parallel bars.

The most important part of the exercise may be the dismount. In the top class of gymnastics, some dazzling and daring descents are now executed off the bar. All of them should end with the performer landing securely on his feet beside the apparatus.

How competitions work

Some people say it is easier to do a handstand on the high bar than to understand the scoring in a big gymnastics competition like the Olympics. However, if you take a deep breath and concentrate like mad, you'll find it is as easy as falling off a beam!

A major gymnastic meeting is held in an arena that is large enough to hold much of the apparatus – floor mat, vaulting horse, pommel horse, rings, balance beam, high bar, parallel bars and asymmetric bars.

The first thing that happens is the team competition. This goes on for two days. On the first day, each of the six members of the team does a compulsory exercise on each piece of apparatus. They are marked out of ten for each exercise. On the second day, they perform voluntary exercises on each piece of apparatus, for which they again receive marks out of ten. The lowest individual mark for each exercise is ignored and all the other marks are added together to make a total score for the compulsory exercises and a total score for the voluntary exercises. These two sets of marks are added

Number One Again! — Nadia Comaneci is triumphant, but it may not be long before the Chinese girls on the right start to catch her up.

together and the team with the highest overall score wins the team competition.

On the next day, the individual competition begins. Every competitor's marks for both compulsory and voluntary exercises are added together and the top 36 gymnasts go through to the individual competition. They each do another voluntary exercise on each piece of apparatus. The score for this final round is added to *half* of their total number of marks from the first two days. The gymnast with the highest score is the champion.

Sorting It Out — If the judges' marks vary too much, the chief judge calls them together for a conference.

The six gymnasts with the highest scores on each piece of apparatus enter for the individual apparatus championship. As in the combined exercises individual competition, the competitor starts out with a preliminary mark which is half the total number of marks from the team event. The gymnast performs voluntary exercises on the apparatus and the mark he or she receives is added to the preliminary mark. The gymnast with most marks on a particular piece of apparatus is the winner of that event.

Modern rhythmic gymnastics

Modern rhythmic gymnastics is a new exciting branch of the sport for girls. It is developing all the time. Like floor exercises, it is performed to music on a floor mat. The routines must include dance steps, jumps, leaps, pivots and balances. The big difference with this branch of gymnastics is that the gymnast can use a rope, hoop, ball, ribbon or clubs. These must move with the gymnast's body as if they were part of it. For example, the ball is bounced and thrown, moved from one hand to the other, and rolled across the body.

It is much harder than it looks. One trick is to throw the rope in the air and catch it again. Points will be lost if the rope becomes slack or if there is any loss of rhythm.

Modern rhythmic gymnastics is the most beautiful of all exercises. It is full of free-flowing movement and graceful dancing. The ribbon exercise is particularly pretty to watch. The satin ribbon twirls and swirls like a snake around her body. The gymnast has a choice of many colours. It is 2.8 m (9½ ft) long, so it is difficult to avoid becoming

Through the Hoop — These girls practising with hoops could soon be training for modern rhythmic gymnastics.

Ribbon Dance — The gymnast above must control the ribbon which moves like a long snake charmed by the music!

tangled up in it.

Team routines are particularly brilliant. They have to include the exchange of equipment between six competitors as they move about. This is a sport that demands perfection – you have to be almost more like a juggler than a gymnast.

That's Not All — Apart from displaying balance, strength and agility, the gymnast on the right has to keep the ball moving.

Sports acrobatics

For sparkling entertainment, nothing beats sports acrobatics. It is a mixture of acrobatics and tumbling. It became internationally organized in 1973.

The gymnast has to run off a 25 metre sprung strip. He gathers up speed as he runs. When the gymnast takes off from the strip, he can reach a tremendous height from which to perform a series of somersaults and twists. There are two exercises. One must include three types of somersault, and the other must include twists of at least 180 degrees. When the best tumblers in the world are in action, the speed and agility is almost unbelievable. The performance of young Soviet gymnast Yuri Zikunov has been described in this way: 'The way this man moves down the tumbling runway can be likened to the take-off of Concorde!'

There are five other events in sports acrobatics and they involve team-work. Pairs of men, women, or a man and a woman perform together. There are also women's trios and men's fours. The largest, strongest member of the team stays at the bottom on

On Top of the World — Vadim Pismenny and Irina Zagorui show off their supremacy as former World mixed pairs champions.

Three's Company — Galina Udodova, Tatiana Tsaenko and Galina Korchemhaya show how it should be done with this spectacular twist in the air.

51

the floor while the smaller members climb
up above him, using each other as support. The trios and fours perform 'human
pyramid' exercises and what are called
'tempo' routines. In these routines bodies are
thrown from one gymnast to another, twisting and somersaulting as they go. Even
gymnasts performing handstands on top of
another gymnast's head seem to be able to
take off with perfect ease.

The Supermen – Vassily Machuga and Vladimir Pochivalov, World men's pairs champions, giving an 'impossible' display in London.

In the men's fours, the pyramid can reach a dizzy height, but it is often the pairs that draw the greatest applause. The Soviet Union has consistently provided the world champions in all sections of sports acrobatics. To see their best pairs in action, you begin to wonder whether they do not have super-bodies! How else could they manage to contort their bodies in such weird positions, or be so strong and controlled?

Trampolining

It did not take circus trapeze artists long to realize that the safety net, into which they could drop if they fell from high apparatus, had possibilities all of its own.

The safety net is very like today's trampoline, which is made of a nylon or canvas sheet or of woven webbing. The bed is stretched by covered springs or elastic cables between a padded metal frame.

You can bounce higher on a trampoline than you can on any other piece of equipment. Advanced trampolinists need about 7.5 m (25 ft) headroom. Outside, you can only trampoline on a perfectly calm day as it is surprising how even a little wind blows you off course.

Trampolining is fun. You can start doing it at a very early age as long as you are supervised. You need at least two spotters with you, one on each side of the bed. When you get going and are bouncing high, the

Nose Dive? — German trampoline star Werner Friedrich heads for the bed, but he'll turn over before landing.

slightest uneven landing can throw you over. A lean of the body to one side, or a leg or arm sticking out, can send you bouncing where you don't want to go.

When that happens, you have to be able to 'kill the bounce' immediately you land, or you can be in trouble. Beginners don't always find this easy but spotters are close by to help you stay on the bed. You have to wear close-fitting clothes and cannot wear jewellery – especially if you are trampolining on a webbing bed, as you might get tangled.

Advanced gymnasts use the trampoline for practising tumbling routines for the floor exercises. It is a world championship sport, with compulsory and voluntary routines. Some of the routines are superb to watch – especially when two gymnasts work on the trampoline at the same time.

Spring in the Air — No trampoline in sight, but how else could Suzy Chaffee fly among the treetops?

Keeping fit

Anyone who wants to be a gymnast must first take his body to school. It needs to be taught to be ready for gymnastics. Real physical fitness is demanded of you – if you are just averagely fit, this is not enough.

You need training. Your coach will see to it that you regularly perform the exercises of bending and stretching that help to give a young body the special suppleness that a gymnast needs. Can you remember watching top gymnasts on the beam practically turning themselves inside out?

But you must make sure that the coach is working on a 'well-oiled machine'. So you should be getting plenty of sleep and cutting out snacks between meals. How many gymnasts have you seen with fat stomachs? They would not get very far if their bodies were not kept in peak condition. Unless you go in to the gym every day, you need to go through a ten-minute routine of simple exercises once a day at home. You should also go on a ten-minute run each day if you can. This will help build up your stamina.

Remember too that you cannot be fit

Dressed to Kill — But not dressed for gymnastics! British Olympic performer Suzanne Dando keeps fit in the garden.

58

Now's Your Chance — The younger you can start gymnastics, the easier it will be to make your body do the work.

unless you are healthy. Do not try to take any violent exercise on days when you don't feel well. Take care of colds and headaches and take special care of your hands and feet which are so important for the gymnast. Always wash your feet after exercise and dry between the toes. Don't ignore scratches –

Far and Wide — A school hall is as good a place as anywhere to learn some routines.

Nadia Comaneci had to withdraw from the World Championships of 1979 because a scratch had become infected.

Above all, take the warm-up period seriously. To stretch cold muscles is certain to bring you the sort of trouble that can keep you out of gymnastics for a long time.

A few things to remember

If you want to be a gymnast, remember that you don't have to be a champion to enjoy gymnastics. It's fun at any level, but the more you put into it – the more you will get out of it. Gymnastics is one of the most perfectly disciplined of all activities. You must always obey the rules of the gym as they are there to stop you getting injured.

Physical talent is not enough to make a good gymnast, not even with physical fitness as well. To master any exercise you have to practise over and over again, sometimes for years. It may be dangerous to attempt new exercises without the approval of your coach, so please wait until you are ready. Enjoy what you are able to do with your body on the various pieces of apparatus when your coach says you can.

Don't Forget! — Alone or with the rest of the club, keep the rules of the gym and always listen to your coach.

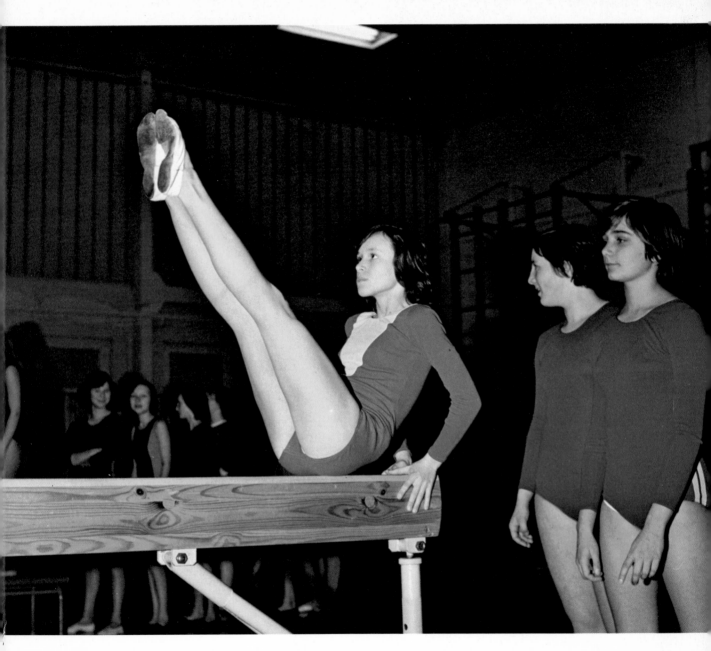

Index

8838

796.4/ Hunn, David
HUN*N*
Gymnastics

$13.00

DATE		
MAR 2 6 1987		
APR 1 6 1987		
MAY 2 1 1987		
APR 6 1995		